Book of
Comfort
&
Healing

INTERFAITH RESOURCES

Interfaith Resources
Book of Comfort and Healing
— Prayers and Inspiration from Many Faiths
Gift Edition

© 2012 Interfaith Resources,
a division of Special Ideas Inc.
Heltonville IN 47436

Compiled by Justice St. Rain and Lynnea Yancy
Suggestions, additions and/or corrections
may be e-mailed to
justice@special-ideas.com

A pocket edition of this booklet can be
purchased in bulk online @
InterfaithResources.com or call 1-800-326-1197
over 40,000 in print

ISBN 978-1-888547-26-X

INTRODUCTION

There are times in every life when the path we walk is steep and rocky. At such times we may feel inadequate to the challenges we face. Worse, we may feel we are traveling alone.

The teachings of the great religions of the world assure us that, no matter what, we are never truly alone. The loving Creator of us all stands ready to hear our complaints and supplications, to bestow guidance, to bless us, to work miracles in our lives, and to comfort us.

If right now you are in need of comfort and healing, we invite you to be open to the guidance, blessings, and miracles in store for you. We hope the verses in this book will help you feel more connected with the Creator; that they will ease the cares of your heart, and will light your way forward.

About the Interfaith nature of this compilation:

These words of comfort
reflect the collected wisdom
of the world's great religious traditions.
We've selected the most universal expressions
possible, avoiding references to specific
religions or their Founders.
We have not been able to avoid the use
of the word "God" or masculine pronouns,
but hope that those who need to can mentally
replace them with whatever Name for the
Transcendent you prefer.
We have used a variety of popular translations,
seeking to find those that are most accessible
to a Western readership.
Please forgive us if a favorite passage
is not translated exactly as you remember it.
The meditations come from sacred texts,
while the prayers come from a variety of sources,
including prayer books, liturgy and internet sites
representing various religious perspectives.

This book is a work in progress.
We welcome suggestions for
additional prayers and writings from any religion,
and accept respectful critiques
of what we have so far.

CONTENTS

God Can Help Us

I lift up my eyes to the hills—where does my help come from? My help comes from the Lord, the Maker of heaven and earth. He will not let your foot slip—He who watches over you will not slumber; Indeed, he who watches over [you] will neither slumber nor sleep. The Lord watches over you—The Lord is your shade at your right hand. The sun will not harm you by day, nor the moon by night. The Lord will keep you from all harm—he will watch over your life; the Lord will watch over your coming and going both now and forever evermore.   — Judaism[1]

I answer the prayer of the suppliant when he crieth unto Me. So let them hear My call and let them trust in Me, in order that they may be led aright.   — Islam[2]

Come to Me, all who labor and are heavy laden, and I will give you rest. Take My yoke upon you, and learn from Me; for I am gentle and lowly in heart, and you will find rest for your souls. For My yoke is easy, and My burden is light.

— Christianity[8]

O thou who art turning thy face toward God! Close thine eyes to all things else, and open them to the realm of the All-Glorious. Ask whatsoever thou wishest of Him alone; seek whatsoever thou seekest from Him alone. With a look He granteth a hundred thousand hopes, with a glance He healeth a hundred thousand incurable ills, with a glimpse He layeth balm on every wound, with a nod He freeth the hearts from the shackles of grief.

— Bahá'í Faith[4]

Night and day, meditate in remembrance on the One who will be your Help and Support in the end.   — Sikhism[5]

The Lord Who is self radiant, existed even before the creation of the universe. He is the only blissful Master of the world. He sustains the earth, the sun, the moon and all the planets. We adore Him with fervent devotion.   — Hinduism[6]

…what can the poor creature do, if the Lord does not give him assistance?   — Sikhism[3]

Ask, and it shall be given you; seek, and ye shall find; knock, and it shall be opened unto you: For every one that asketh receiveth; and he that seeketh findeth; and to him that knocketh it shall be opened.   — Christianity[7]

Sing the Glories of God each and every day; your afflictions shall be dispelled, and you shall be saved, my humble friend.   — Sikhism[9]

Remember ye implored the assistance of your Lord, and He answered you: "I will assist you with a thousand of the angels, ranks on ranks."
                                    — Islam[10]

Prayers for Assistance

O Lord! Thou art the Remover of every anguish and the Dispeller of every afflication. Thou art He Who banisheth every sorrow and setteth free every slave, the Redeemer of every soul. O Lord! Grant deliverance through Thy mercy, and reckon me among such servants of Thine as have gained salvation. — Bahá'í Faith[11]

O God, the Strength of the weak, the Comfort of the sorrowful, the Friend of the lonely: let not sorrow overwhelm Thy children, nor anguish of heart turn them from Thee. Grant that in the patience of hope…they may continue in Thy service and in all godly living, until at length they also attain unto fullness of life before Thy face…
— Christianity[12]

There is none as forlorn as I am, and none as Compassionate as You; what need is there to test us now? May my mind surrender to Your Word; please, bless Your humble servant with this perfection.   — Sikhism[13]

O Lord in Thee may all be happy. May all be free from misery. May all realize goodness and may no one suffer pain.

— Hinduism[14]

Is there any remover of difficulties save God? Say: Praised be God. He is God. All are His servants and all abide by His bidding.

— Bahá'í Faith[15]

O Father of the Earth, by fixed laws ruling,
O Father of the Heavens, pray protect us,
O Father of the great and shining Waters!
What God shall we adore with our oblation?
O Lord of creatures, Father of all beings,
You alone pervade all that has come to birth.
Grant us our heart's desire for which we pray.
May we become the Lords of many treasures!

— Hinduism[16]

Just as the soft rains fill the streams,
pour into the rivers and join together in the
oceans, so may the power of every moment of
your goodness flow forth to awaken and heal all
beings, those here now, those gone before,
those yet to come.
By the power of every moment of your goodness, may your heart's wishes be soon fulfilled
as completely shining as the bright full moon,
as magically as by a wish-fulfilling gem.
By the power of every moment of your goodness
may all dangers be averted and all disease be
gone.
May no obstacle come across your way.
May you enjoy fulfillment and long life.
For all in whose heart dwells respect, who
follow the wisdom and compassion of the Way,
May your life prosper in the four blessings
of old age, beauty, happiness and strength.

— Buddhism[17]

God Loves Us

God is love. — Christianity[18]

And God saw every thing that he had made, and, behold, it was very good. — Christianity[19]

O SON OF MAN! Veiled in My immemorial being and in the ancient eternity of My essence, I knew My love for thee; therefore I created thee, have engraved on thee Mine image and revealed to thee My beauty.

O SON OF MAN! I loved thy creation, hence I created thee. Wherefore, do thou love Me, that I may name thy name and fill thy soul with the spirit of life. — Bahá'í Faith[20]

The Lord God is my Friend and Companion. God shall be my Helper and Support in the end. — Sikhism[21]

I am alike for all! I know not hate, I know not favour! What is made is Mine! But them that worship Me with love, I love; They are in Me, and I in them!   — Hinduism[22]

Take My last word, My utmost meaning have! Precious thou art to Me; right well-beloved! Listen! I tell thee for thy comfort this. Give Me thy heart! adore Me! serve Me! Cling in faith and love and reverence to Me! So shalt thou come to Me! I promise true, For thou art sweet to Me!
                              — Hinduism[23]

The Lord and Cherisher of the Worlds; Who created me, and it is He Who guides me; Who gives me food and drink, And when I am ill, it is He Who cures me; Who will cause me to die, and then to live again; And Who, I hope, will forgive me my faults on the Day of Judgment...
                              — Islam[24]

The Lord is gracious and full of compassion, slow to anger, and of great mercy. The Lord is good to all and His tender mercies are over all His works.   — Judaism[25]

Consider the lilies how they grow: they toil not, they spin not; and yet I say unto you, that Solomon in all his glory was not arrayed like one of these. If then God so clothe the grass, which is today in the field, and tomorrow is cast into the oven; how much more will he clothe you, O ye of little faith? And seek not ye what ye shall eat, or what ye shall drink, neither be ye of doubtful mind. For all these things do the nations of the world seek after: and your Father knoweth that ye have need of these things. But rather seek ye the kingdom of God; and all these things shall be added unto you.

— Christianity[26]

Yea! knowing Me the source of all, by Me all creatures wrought, The wise in spirit cleave to Me, into My Being brought; Hearts fixed on Me; breaths breathed to Me; praising Me, each to each, So have they happiness and peace, with pious thought and speech; And unto these—thus serving well, thus loving ceaselessly—I give a mind of perfect mood, whereby they draw to Me; And, all for love of them, within their darkened souls I dwell, And, with bright rays of wisdom's lamp, their ignorance dispel.　　　— Hinduism[27]

...and wants us to be happy

Be happy and joyous because the bestowals of God are intended for you and the life of the Holy Spirit is breathing upon you.

Rejoice, for the heavenly table is prepared for you.

Rejoice, for the angels of heaven are your assistants and helpers. — Bahá'í Faith[28]

Make a joyful noise unto the Lord, all ye lands. Serve the Lord with gladness: come before his presence with singing. Know ye that the Lord he is God: it is he that hath made us, and not we ourselves; we are his people, and the sheep of his pasture.

Enter into his gates with thanksgiving, and into his courts with praise: be thankful unto him, and bless his name. For the Lord is good; his mercy is everlasting; and his truth endureth to all generations. I will sing of mercy and judgment: unto thee, O Lord, will I sing. — Judaism[29]

Those who believe and do right: Joy is for them, and bliss (their) journey's end. — Islam[30]

The virtuous find joy in this world, and they find joy in the next; they find joy in both. They find joy and are glad when they see the good they have done. — Buddhism[31]

Make Me your supremest joy! and, undivided, Unto My rest your spirits shall be guided.
— Hinduism[32]

Prayers for Those We Love

Love of God

I worship you in every religion that teaches your laws and praises your glory. I worship you in every plant whose beauty reflects your beauty. I worship you in every event which is caused by your goodness and kindness. I worship you in every place where you dwell. And I worship you in every man and woman who seeks to follow your way of righteousness. — Zoroastrianism[33]

O Thou who acceptest penitent acts. Thou who art greatly beneficent. Thou who hearkenest unto those who call. Thou who knowest hidden things. O thou before whose greatness everything is humbled. O thou before whom everything bows in awe. O thou by whose command the heavens and the earth abide. O thou in whose fear all things obey. Thou goal of hopes: thou refuge of every outcast. O Master of the covenant and promise. O thou who bestowest our requests. O thou who discoverest the distress of every weary soul.

O thou who concealest every blemished thing. O thou companion of every lonely soul. O thou who befriendest me in my solitariness. O thou who companionest me in my loneliness. O thou who art faithful in covenant. O thou who bestowest our desires. O Lord of majesty and power. — Islam[34]

Prayers for Children and Youth

O Thou peerless Lord! Let this suckling babe be nursed from the breast of Thy loving-kindness, guard it within the cradle of Thy safety and protection and grant that it be reared in the arms of Thy tender affection. — Bahá'í Faith[35]

Heavenly Father, my child is your greatest gift, and my biggest challenge! I know my child is truly distressed, and yet I am at my wit's end to find a peaceful resolution. I feel helpless and frustrated. I ask myself, What would my Heavenly Father do in His infinite wisdom and beneficence? Lord, come into my heart and mind, and share Your loving wisdom with me! Help my child to heal his pain, and help me to become as loving and wise a parent, as You are for us Your children. Thank You Lord, for hearing me and coming to my aid! Bring your loving Peace to me and my child today. — Christianity[36]

O Thou kind Lord! These lovely children are the handiwork of the fingers of Thy might and the wondrous signs of Thy greatness. O God! Protect these children, graciously assist them to be educated and enable them to render service to the world of humanity. O God! These children are pearls, cause them to be nurtured within the shell of Thy loving-kindness.

Thou art the Bountiful, the All-Loving.

— Bahá'í Faith[37]

A Father's Prayer for his Family

Lord, Grant us joy of our wives and children. Make reverence the garment of our love and hallowing the benediction of our homes. By the surety of the troth we keep make safe the troths of all. For the joy of our eyes grant us faith in our souls. Make us and ours ready for all seasons, gay and grave. Make our loves true and in their truth make our nation glad. Lord, hear our prayer: our prayer, Lord, hear. Amen.   — Christianity [38]

Prayers for Parents

Thou seest, O Lord, our suppliant hands lifted up towards the heaven of Thy favour and bounty. Grant that they may be filled with the treasures of Thy munificence and bountiful favours. Forgive us, and our fathers and our mothers, and fulfill whatsoever we have desired from the ocean of Thy grace and Divine generosity. Accept, O Beloved of our hearts all our works in Thy path. Thou art, verily, the Most Powerful, the Most Exalted, the Incomparable, the One, the Forgiving, the Gracious. — Bahá'í Faith [39]

It is seemly that the servant should, after each prayer, supplicate God to bestow mercy and forgiveness upon his parents. Thereupon God's call will be raised: "Thousand upon thousand of what thou hast asked for thy parents shall be thy recompense!" Blessed is he who remembereth his parents when communing with God. There is, verily, no God but Him, the Mighty, the Well-Beloved.

— Bahá'í Faith[40]

Prayer for Expectant Mothers

My Lord! My Lord! I praise Thee and I thank Thee for that whereby Thou hast favored Thine humble maidservant, Thy slave beseeching and supplicating Thee, because Thou hast verily guided her unto Thine obvious Kingdom and caused her to hear thine exalted Call in the contingent world and to behold thy Signs which prove the appearance of Thy victorious reign over all things.

O my Lord, I dedicate that which is in my womb unto Thee. Then cause it to be a praiseworthy child in Thy Kingdom and fortunate one by Thy favor and Thy generosity; to develop and to grow up under the charge of Thine education. Verily, Thou art the Gracious! Verily, Thou art the Lord of Great Favor!   — Bahá'í Faith[41]

God Guides Us

Nothing happens to you except in accordance with God's will. Anyone who believes in God, He will guide his heart. God is fully aware of all things.

— Islam[42]

If you will listen carefully to the voice of the Lord your God, and do what is right in his sight, and give heed to his commandments and keep all his statutes, I will not bring upon you any of the diseases that I brought upon the Egyptians; for I am the Lord who heals you.   — Judaism[43]

People should keep these Truths clearly in mind, for the world is filled with suffering and if anyone wishes to escape from suffering, he must sever the ties of worldly passion which is the sole cause of suffering. The way of life which is free from all worldly passion and suffering can only be known through Enlightenment....

— Buddhism [44]

Those humble beings who struggle with their minds are brave and distinguished heroes. Those who realize their own selves, remain forever united with the Lord. This is the glory of the spiritual teachers, that they remain absorbed in their mind. They attain the Mansion of the Lord's Presence, and focus their meditation on the True Lord. Those who conquer their own minds...conquer the world.   — Sikhism [45]

The Prophets and Messengers of God have been sent down for the sole purpose of guiding mankind to the straight Path of Truth.

—Bahá'í Faith[46]

Prayers for Guidance

Grant to me, O Lord, to know what I ought to know, to love what I ought to love, to praise what delights Thee most, to value what is precious in Thy sight, to hate what is offensive to Thee. Do not suffer me to judge according to the sight of my eyes, nor to pass sentence according to the hearing of the ears of ignorant men; but to discern with true judgment between things visible and spiritual, and above all things to enquire what is the good pleasure of Thy will.

— Christianity [47]

In the Name of God, Most Gracious, Most Merciful, Praise be to God, the Cherisher and Sustainer of the two worlds, Most Gracious, Most Merciful, Master of the Day of Judgment. Thee do we worship and Thine aid do we seek, Show us the straight path, the path of those upon whom Thou hast bestowed Thy grace, those whose portion is not wrath, and who go not astray.   — Islam[48]

Heavenly Father, who graciously bestowest knowledge on man and endowest him with reason, send us the light of Thy truth, that we may gain an ever clearer insight into the wisdom of Thy ways. Banish from our hearts every desire and thought of evil, that we may truly revere Thy holy name. Forgive our sins, pardon our failings, and remove from us suffering and sorrow. May the erring and the wayward be led to know Thy loving kindness, and to serve Thee in a newness of heart; and may those who love virtue and do the right, ever be glad of Thy favor. Bless our land with plenty and our nation with peace; may righteousness dwell in our midst and virtue reign among us.

O Thou, who knowest our needs before we utter them, and ordainest all things for the best, in Thee do we forever put our trust.

— Judaism[49]

I adjure Thee by Thy might, O my God! Let no harm beset me in times of tests, and in moments of heedlessness guide my steps aright through Thine inspiration. Thou art God, potent art Thou to do what Thou desirest. No one can withstand Thy Will or thwart Thy Purpose.

— Bahá'í Faith[50]

O Lord you are the Giver of life, Remover of pains and sorrows, Bestower of happiness. May we receive the supreme sin-destroying light of the Creator of the universe. May You guide our intellect in the right direction. — Hinduism[51]

We pray to God to eradicate all the misery in the world: that understanding triumph over ignorance, that generosity triumphs over indifference, that trust triumphs over contempt, and that truth triumphs over falsehood.

— Zoroastrianism[52]

O God! We are weak; give us strength. We are poor; bestow upon us Thine illimitable treasures. We are sick; grant unto us Thy divine healing. We are impotent; give us Thy heavenly power. O Lord! Make us useful in this world; free us from the condition of self and desire. O Lord! Make us brethren in Thy love, and cause us to be loving toward all Thy children. Confirm us in service to the world of humanity so that we may become the servants of Thy servants, that we may love all Thy creatures and become compassionate to all Thy people. O Lord, Thou art the Almighty. Thou art the Merciful. Thou art the Forgiver. Thou art the Omnipotent. — Bahá'í Faith[53]

God Forgives Us

Say: If ye love God, then follow me: God will love you, and forgive your sins, for God is Forgiving, Merciful. — Islam[54]

Verily I say unto you, All sins shall be forgiven unto the sons of men.... — Christianity[55]

Seek ye the Lord while he may be found, call ye upon him while he is near: Let the wicked forsake his way, and the unrighteous man his thoughts: and let him return unto the Lord, and he will have mercy upon him; and to our God, for he will abundantly pardon. — Judaism[56]

Fly to Me alone! Make Me thy single refuge! I will free Thy soul from all its sins! Be of good cheer! — Hinduism[57]

Thou art the All-Merciful, and verily Thou art the Ever-Forgiving, He to Whom repentance is due, He Who forgiveth even the most grievous of sins. — Bahá'í Faith[58]

Prayers for Forgiveness

Our Father, which art in heaven, hallowed be thy name. Thy kingdom come, Thy will be done in earth, as it is in heaven. Give us this day our daily bread. And forgive us our debts, as we forgive our debtors. And lead us not into temptation, but deliver us from evil: For thine is the kingdom, and the power, and the glory, for ever. Amen.

— Christianity[59]

Look, we beseech thee, and speedily have mercy upon the people for thy name's sake in thine abundant mercies. O Lord our God, spare and be merciful: save the sheep of thy pasture; let not wrath rule over us, for our eyes are bent upon thee; save us for thy name's sake. Have mercy upon us for the sake of thy covenant; look and answer us in time of trouble, for salvation is thine, O Lord.

— Judaism[60]

O our Lord, take us not to task, if we forget or miss the mark. O our Lord, lay not on us a burden like that which thou didst lay on those before us. O our Lord, lay not on us that which we have no strength to carry. Pardon us and forgive us. Thou art our Master. — Islam[61]

Mine eyes are ever toward the Lord; for he shall pluck my feet out of the net. Turn thee unto me, and have mercy upon me; for I am desolate and afflicted. The troubles of my heart are enlarged: O bring thou me out of my distresses. Look upon mine affliction and my pain; and forgive all my sins…. Let integrity and uprightness preserve me; for I wait on thee. — Judaism[62]

O Lord! Thou art the Remover of every anguish and the Dispeller of every affliction. Thou art He Who banisheth every sorrow and setteth free every slave, the Redeemer of every soul. O Lord! Grant deliverance through Thy mercy, and reckon me among such servants of Thine as have gained salvation. — Bahá'í Faith[63]

O Thou forgiving Lord! Thou art the shelter of all these Thy servants. Thou knowest the secrets and art aware of all things. We are all helpless, and Thou art the Mighty, the Omnipotent. We are all sinners, and Thou art the Forgiver of sins, the Merciful, the Compassionate. O Lord! Look not at our shortcomings. Deal with us according to Thy grace and bounty. Our shortcomings are many, but the ocean of Thy forgiveness is boundless. Our weakness is grievous, but the evidences of Thine aid and assistance are clear. Therefore, confirm and strengthen us. Enable us to do that which is worthy of Thy holy Threshold. Illumine our hearts, grant us discerning eyes and attentive ears. Resuscitate the dead and heal the sick. Bestow wealth upon the poor and give peace and security to the fearful. Accept us in Thy kingdom and illumine us with the light of guidance. Thou are the Powerful and the Omnipotent. Thou art the Generous. Thou art the Clement. Thou art the Kind.

— Bahá'í Faith[64]

God Protects Us

The Lord is my light and my salvation: whom shall I fear?

— Judaism [65]

All that is in Heaven and all that is in Earth is God's! God is a sufficient protector!   —Islam [66]

Let the fear of no one dismay thee. Trust in the Lord, thy God, for He is sufficient unto whosoever trusteth in Him. He, verily, shall protect thee, and in Him shalt thou abide in safety.

— Bahá'í Faith [67]

But whoso hearkeneth unto me shall dwell safely, and shall be quiet from fear of evil.

— Judaism [68]

He is God than whom there is no god; who knows the unseen and the visible; He is the merciful, the compassionate! He is God than whom there is no god; the King, the Holy, the Peace-Giver, the Faithful, the Protector, the Mighty, the Repairer, the Great!

— Islam[69]

O SON OF BEING!

My love is My stronghold; he that entereth therein is safe and secure, and he that turneth away shall surely stray and perish.

— Bahá'í Faith[70]

All sorrow comes from fear. From nothing else. When you know this, You become free of it, And desire melts away. You become happy And still.

— Hinduism[71]

Prayers for Protection

In Thee, O Lord, have I taken refuge; let me never be ashamed; Deliver me in Thy righteousness. Incline Thine ear unto me, deliver me speedily; Be Thou to me a rock of refuge, even a fortress of defense, to save me. For Thou art my rock and my fortress; Therefore for Thy name's sake lead me and guide me. Bring me forth out of the net that they have hidden for me; For Thou art my stronghold. Into Thy hand I commit my spirit; Thou hast redeemed me, O Lord, Thou God of truth. — Judaism [72]

O Destroyer of pain, Bestower of Mercy, Fascinating Lord, Destroyer of sorrow and strife, I have come to Your Sanctuary; please preserve my honor. You are all-pervading, O Immaculate Lord. He hears and beholds all; God is with us, the nearest of the near.

—Sikhism[73]

We know thee Lord of ample store, to thee have sent our hearts' desires: be therefore our Protector thou.   — Hinduism[74]

O my Lord! Thou knowest that the people are encircled with pain and calamities and are environed with hardships and trouble. Every trial doth attack man and every dire adversity doth assail him like unto the assault of a serpent. There is no shelter and asylum for him except under the wing of Thy protection, preservation, guard and custody.

O Thou the Merciful One! O my Lord! Make Thy protection my armor, Thy preservation my shield, humbleness before the door of Thy oneness my guard, and Thy custody and defense my fortress and my abode. Preserve me from the suggestions of self and desire, and guard me from every sickness, trial, difficulty and ordeal.

Verily, Thou art the Protector, the Guardian, the Preserver, the Sufficer, and verily, Thou art the Merciful of the Most Merciful.

                                    — Bahá'í Faith[75]

Lighten our darkness, we beseech thee, O Lord, and by thy great mercy defend us from all perils and dangers of this night.

— Christianity[76]

Immeasurably exalted art Thou, O Lord! Protect us from what licth in front of us and behind us, above our heads, on our right, on our left, below our feet and every other side to which we are exposed. Verily, Thy protection over all things is unfailing.

— Bahá'í Faith[77]

O self-radiant and omnipresent God, You are the ultimate Reality pervading the entire universe. You protect the innocent... May we be provided with the strength to fight and drive away disease, suffering, evil and sin. Whatever I own is for You, my Lord; it is not for myself.

— Hinduism[78]

God Heals Us

And when I am ill, it is He Who cures me...
— Islam[79]

For I will restore health unto thee, and I will heal thee of thy wounds, saith the Lord....
— Judaism[80]

The Love of the Lord is the healing remedy; the Name of the Lord is the healing remedy.
— Sikhism[81]

Thy Name is my healing, O my God, and remembrance of Thee is my remedy.
— Bahá'í Faith[82]

I am the Keeper; I am the Creator and the Maintainer; I am the Discerner; I am the most Beneficent Spirit. My name is the bestower of health; my name is the best bestower of health.
— Zoroastrianism[83]

O Lord my God, I cried unto thee, and thou hast healed me. — Judaism [84]

O mind, there is only the One medicine, mantra and healing herb—center your consciousness firmly on the One Lord. — Sikhism [85]

God Heals through Prayer

Is any among you afflicted? let him pray. Is any merry? let him sing psalms. Is any sick among you? let him call for the elders of the church; and let them pray over him, anointing him with oil in the name of the Lord: And the prayer of faith shall save the sick, and the Lord shall raise him up; and if he have committed sins, they shall be forgiven him. Confess your faults one to another, and pray one for another, that ye may be healed. The effectual fervent prayer of a righteous man availeth much.

— Christianity[86]

Meditating, meditating in remembrance on my Lord and Master, I became cool and calm; my pains, sorrows and doubts are gone. Whoever has been saved in the past or the present, was saved through loving devotional worship of the Divine Lord. — Sikhism[87]

Then they cried to the Lord in their trouble, and he saved them from their distress; he sent out his word and healed them, and delivered them from destruction. Let them thank the Lord for his steadfast love, for his wonderful works to humankind. — Judaism[88]

God Heals through Medicine

There are two ways of healing sickness, material means and spiritual means. The first is by the treatment of physicians; the second consisteth in prayers offered by the spiritual ones to God and in turning to Him. Both means should be used and practiced. Illnesses which occur by reason of physical causes should be treated by doctors with medical remedies; those which are due to spiritual causes disappear through spiritual means. Thus an illness caused by affliction, fear, nervous impressions, will be healed more effectively by spiritual rather than by physical treatment. Hence, both kinds of treatment should be followed; they are not contradictory.... — Bahá'í Faith[89]

One may heal with Holiness, one may heal with the Law, one may heal with the knife, one may heal with herbs, one may heal with the Holy Word: amongst all remedies this one is the healing one that heals with the Holy Word; this one it is that will best drive away sickness from the body of the faithful: for this one is the best healing of all remedies. — Zoroastrianism[90]

Physician's Prayer

Lord, Thou Great Physician, I kneel before Thee. Since every good and perfect gift must come from Thee, I Pray: Give skill to my hand, clear vision to my mind, kindness and sympathy to my heart. Give me singleness of purpose, strength to lift at least a part of the burden of my suffering fellow men, and a true realization of the rare privilege that is mine. Take from my heart all guile and worldliness, that with the simple faith of a child I may rely on Thee. — Interfaith[91]

God Heals through Us

If you do not tend to one another, then who is there to tend you? Whoever would tend Me, he should tend the sick.   — Buddhism[92]

Pleasant words are as an honeycomb, sweet to the soul, and health to the bones.   — Judaism[93]

Matters related to man's spirit have a great effect on his bodily condition. For instance, thou shouldst impart gladness to thy patient, give him comfort and joy, and bring him to ecstasy and exultation. How often hath it occurred that this hath caused early recovery. Therefore, treat thou the sick with both powers [physical and spiritual]. Spiritual feelings have a surprising effect on healing nervous ailments.

...Remedy the sick by means of heavenly joy and spiritual exultation, cure the sorely afflicted by imparting to them blissful glad tidings and heal the wounded through His resplendent bestowals. When at the bedside of a patient, cheer and gladden his heart and enrapture his spirit through celestial power. Indeed, such a heavenly breath quickeneth every mouldering bone and reviveth the spirit of every sick and ailing one.

— Bahá'í Faith[94]

Prayers for Healing

The prayers which were revealed to ask for healing apply both to physical and spiritual healing. Recite them, then, to heal both the soul and the body. If healing is right for the patient, it will certainly be granted; but for some ailing persons, healing would only be the cause of other ills, and therefore wisdom doth not permit an affirmative answer to the prayer.

— Bahá'í Faith[95]

Heal us, Lord, and we shall be healed; save us, and we shall be saved; for it is You we praise. Send relief and healing for all our diseases, our sufferings and our wounds; for You are a merciful and faithful healer. Blessed are You Lord, who heals the sick. — Judaism[96]

O God, remove the hardship, O Lord of mankind, grant cure for You are the Healer. There is no cure but from You, a cure which leaves no illness behind. — Islam[97]

Thy Name is my healing, O my God, and remembrance of Thee is my remedy. Nearness to Thee is my hope, and love for Thee is my companion. Thy mercy to me is my healing and my succor in both this world and the world to come. Thou, verily, art the All-Bountiful, the All-Knowing, the All-Wise.   — Bahá'í Faith[98]

Your Name, O Transcendent Lord, is Ambrosial Nectar; whoever meditates on it, lives. One who is blessed with God's Grace—that humble servant becomes immaculate and pure. Obstacles are removed, and all pains are eliminated....
                          — Sikhism[99]

Heavenly Father, You are intimately aware of the struggle I am experiencing—the pain and the despair. You know the desire of my heart to be healed of this illness. I ask now for Your healing touch. I know that You are able...You can heal me.

I also understand that You will chose what is best for me. I pray that through this trial, I will draw close to You—that You will be my comfort and strength. I pray that ultimately, whatever happens, You will be glorified through me.
                          — Christianity[100]

O almighty God, may my tongue be ever-blessed with the power of speech, may my nostrils be blessed with healthy and vital air, may my eyes be blessed with the perfect power of sight, ears with the perfect power of hearing, arms with strength, legs with vitality. May all the parts of my body be in perfect health....

— Hinduism[101]

May all beings everywhere plagued with sufferings of body and mind quickly be freed from their illnesses. May those frightened cease to be afraid, and may those bound be free. May the powerless find power, and may people think of befriending one another. May those who find themselves in trackless, fearful wilderness—the children, the aged, the unprotected—be guarded by beneficent celestials, and may they swiftly attain enlightenment.

—Buddhism[102]

O God I beseech You to give me health and happiness at the earliest, make me survive misfortunes, and let me depart from the world only unto Your mercy.   —Islam[103]

O God, my God! I beg of Thee by the ocean of Thy healing, and by the splendors of the Day-Star of Thy grace, and by Thy Name through which Thou didst subdue Thy servants, and by the pervasive power of Thy most exalted Word and the potency of Thy most august Pen, and by Thy mercy that hath preceded the creation of all who are in heaven and on earth, to purge me with the waters of Thy bounty from every affliction and disorder, and from all weakness and feebleness.

Thou seest, O my Lord, Thy suppliant waiting at the door of Thy bounty, and him who hath set his hopes on Thee clinging to the cord of Thy generosity. Deny him not, I beseech Thee, the things he seeketh from the ocean of Thy grace and the Day-Star of Thy loving-kindness.

Powerful art Thou to do what pleaseth Thee. There is none other God save Thee, the Ever-Forgiving, the Most Generous.

— Bahá'í Faith[104]

Lord, look upon me with eyes of mercy, may your healing hand rest upon me, may your life-giving powers flow into every cell of my body and into the depths of my soul, cleansing, purifying, restoring me to wholeness and strength for service in your Kingdom.   — Christianity[105]

O Lord God, make me whole, in body, in hearing and in seeing. There is no God save thee. I beseech thee, Lord, let it be well with me beyond the judgment. I ask thee life beyond the grave and the blessed vision of thy gracious Face, yearning to behold thee, all hurtful ill apart, all devious evil spent. I seek refuge with thee from wrongdoing and from being wronged, from enmity within me and against me, and lest I come by any sin or guilt thou pardonest not. — Islam[106]

I am but a poor creature, O my Lord; I have clung to the hem of Thy riches. I am sore sick; I have held fast the cord of Thy healing. Deliver me from the ills that have encircled me, and wash me thoroughly with the waters of Thy graciousness and mercy, and attire me with the raiment of wholesomeness, through Thy forgiveness and bounty. Fix, then, mine eyes upon Thee, and rid me of all attachment to aught else except Thyself. Aid me to do what Thou desirest, and to fulfill what Thou pleasest.

Thou art truly the Lord of this life and of the next. Thou art, in truth, the Ever-Forgiving, the Most Merciful.

— Bahá'í Faith[107]

O God, make me healthy with Your remedy, cure me with Your medicine, keep me safe from the misfortunes with which You try me, because verily I am Your servant, the son of Your servant.

— Islam[108]

Have mercy upon me, O Lord; for I am weak: O Lord, heal me; for my bones are vexed.

— Judaism[109]

Beloved Lord, Almighty God! Through the rays of the sun, through the waves of the air, through the All-pervading Life in space, purify and revivify me, and I pray heal my body, heart, and soul.

— Sufi[110]

God Tests Us

We rejoice in our sufferings, knowing that suffering produces endurance, and endurance produces character, and character produces hope, and hope does not disappoint us, because God's love has been poured into our hearts.

— Christianity[111]

It is under the greatest adversity that there exists the greatest potential for doing good, both for oneself and others.

— Buddhism[112]

We will try you with something of fear, and hunger and loss of wealth, and souls and fruit; but give good tidings to the patient, who when there falls on them a calamity say, "Verily, we are God's and, verily, to Him do we return." These, on them are blessings from their Lord and mercy, and they it is who are guided.

— Islam[113]

And though the Lord give you the bread of adversity, and the water of affliction, yet shall not thy teachers be removed into a corner any more, but thine eyes shall see thy teachers: And thine ears shall hear a word behind thee, saying, This is the way, walk ye in it, when ye turn to the right hand, and when ye turn to the left.

— Judaism[114]

How rare are those humble beings in this world, whom the Lord tests and places in His Treasury. They rise above social status and color, and rid themselves of possessiveness and greed.

— Sikhism[115]

God Tests Us Because God Loves Us

…the Lord tests us, and blesses us with His Glance of Grace.　　　— Sikhism[116]

The more difficulties one sees in the world the more perfect one becomes…. The more you put the gold in the fire the purer it becomes. The more you sharpen the steel by grinding the better it cuts. Therefore, the more sorrows one sees the more perfect one becomes. That is why, in all times, the Prophets of God have had tribulations and difficulties to withstand. The more often the

captain of a ship is in the tempest and difficult sailing the greater his knowledge becomes. Therefore I am happy that you have had great tribulations and difficulties. For this I am very happy—that you have had many sorrows. Strange it is that I love you and still I am happy that you have sorrows. — Bahá'í Faith[117]

God Tests Our Patience

O you who believe, seek help with patience and prayers, as God is with those who patiently persevere. — Islam[118]

My brethren, count it all joy when ye fall into divers temptations; Knowing this, that the trying of your faith worketh patience. But let patience have her perfect work, that ye may be perfect and entire, wanting nothing. — Christianity[119]

Blessed are the steadfastly enduring, they that are patient under ills and hardships, who lament not over anything that befalleth them, and who tread the path of resignation....
— Bahá'í Faith[120]

God Tests Our Detachment

If by giving up a small pleasure, one sees a great pleasure, the wise will let go of the small pleasure and look to the great one.

— Buddhism[121]

The gold is touched to the touchstone, and tested by fire; when its pure color shows through, it is pleasing to the eye of the assayer.

— Sikhism[122]

...The mind and spirit of man advance when he is tried by suffering. The more the ground is plowed the better the seed will grow, the better the harvest will be. Just as the plough furrows the earth deeply, purifying it of weeds and thistles, so suffering and tribulation free man from the petty affairs of this worldly life until he arrives at a state of complete detachment. His attitude in this world will be that of divine happiness. Man is, so to speak, unripe: the heat of the fire of suffering will mature him. Look back to the times past and you will find that the greatest men have suffered most.   — Bahá'í Faith[123]

That man alone is wise who keeps the mastery of himself! ...if one deals with objects of the sense not loving and not hating, making them serve his free soul, which rests serenely, Lord, Lo! such a man comes to tranquillity; and out of that tranquillity shall rise the end and healing of his earthly pains, since the will governed sets the soul at peace.   — Hinduism[124]

When you are plagued by great and excessive anxiety, and diseases of the body; when you are wrapped up in the attachments of household and family, sometimes feeling joy, and then other times sorrow; when you are wandering around in all four directions, and you cannot sit or sleep even for a moment—if you come to remember the Supreme Lord God, then your body and mind shall be cooled and soothed.   —Sikhism[125]

Verily the most necessary thing is contentment under all circumstances; by this one is preserved from morbid conditions and from lassitude. Yield not to grief and sorrow: they cause the greatest misery.   — Bahá'í Faith[126]

Encountering sufferings will definitely contribute to the elevation of your spiritual practice, provided you are able to transform calamity and misfortune into the path. — Buddhism[127]

All things arise, Suffer change, And pass away. This is their nature. When you know this, Nothing perturbs you, Nothing hurts you. You become still. It is easy. — Hinduism[128]

A cheerful heart is a good medicine.
— Judaism[129]

...one who is content to be content may always be content. — Taoism[130]

God Tests Our Faith

Do men imagine that they will be left because they say, "We believe," and will not be tested with affliction? Lo! We tested those who were before you. Thus God knows those who are sincere, and knows those who feign.   — Islam[131]

For verily I say unto you, That whosoever shall say unto this mountain, Be thou removed, and be thou cast into the sea; and shall not doubt in his heart, but shall believe that those things which he saith shall come to pass; he shall have whatsoever he saith. Therefore I say unto you, What things soever ye desire, when ye pray, believe that ye receive them, and ye shall have them.
                    — Christianity[132]

There is a saying in Tibetan, "Tragedy should be utilized as a source of strength." No matter what sort of difficulties, how painful experience is, if we lose our hope, that's our real disaster.
                    — Buddhism[133]

While a man is happy he may forget his God; but when grief comes and sorrows overwhelm him, then will he remember his Father who is in Heaven, and who is able to deliver him from his humiliations. Men who suffer not, attain no perfection. The plant most pruned by the gardeners is that one which, when the summer comes, will have the most beautiful blossoms and the most abundant fruit. The labourer cuts up the earth with his plough, and from that earth comes the rich and plentiful harvest. The more a man is chastened, the greater is the harvest of spiritual virtues shown forth by him.   — Bahá'í Faith[134]

God Tests Our Compassion

I have found that the greatest degree of inner tranquility comes from the development of love and compassion. The more we care for the happiness of others, the greater is our own sense of well-being. Cultivating a close, warm-hearted feeling for others automatically puts the mind at ease. It is the ultimate source of success in life.

—Buddhism[135]

Come, you who are blessed by my Father; take your inheritance, the kingdom prepared for you since the creation of the world. For I was hungry and you gave me something to eat, … I was sick and you looked after me, I was in prison and you came to visit me.

Then the righteous will answer him, "Lord, when did we see you hungry and feed you, … When did we see you sick or in prison and go to visit you?"

The King will reply, "I tell you the truth, whatever you did for one of the least of these brothers of mine, you did for me."

— Christianity[136]

We should all visit the sick. When they are in sorrow and suffering, it is a real help and benefit to have a friend come. Happiness is a great healer to those who are ill. In the East it is the custom to call upon the patient often and meet him individually. The people in the East show the utmost kindness and compassion to the sick and suffering. This has greater effect than the remedy itself. You must always have this thought of love and affection when you visit the ailing and afflicted.

— Bahá'í Faith[137]

Prayers for Assistance with Tests

O God, my only plea is my plight, all I have to offer is my lack. My intercessor is my tears, my treasure is my frailty. O my God, a drop from the ocean of your glory will suffice me. Have mercy upon me, provide me, pardon me and it will be pardoned me. Breathe on my sorrow and make glad my stress and strain by your mercy, the ever All-Merciful.   — Islam[138]

O God! The trials Thou sendest are a salve to the sores of all them who are devoted to Thy will; the remembrance of Thee is a healing medicine to the hearts of such as have drawn nigh unto Thy court; nearness to Thee is the true life of them who are Thy lovers; Thy presence is the ardent desire of such as yearn to behold Thy face; remoteness from Thee is a torment to those that have acknowledged Thy oneness, and separation from Thee is death unto them that have recognized Thy truth!   — Bahá'í Faith[139]

Lighten our darkness, we beseech thee, O Lord, and by thy great mercy defend us from all perils and dangers of this night. — Christianity[140]

O Son of Strength, clad in the robe of riches, may we escape from woe as from a prison.
— Hinduism[141]

My help in poverty, my refuge in distress. My restorer in faintheartedness, my healer in distraction. O thou who makest an end of evil deeds. O thou in whom every complaint comes to an end.
— Islam[142]

Save me, O God, for the waters have come up to my neck. I sink in the miry depths, where there is no foothold. I have come into the deep waters; the floods engulf me. I am worn out calling for help; my throat is parched. My eyes fail, looking for my God... But I pray to you, O Lord, in the time of your favor; In your great love, O God, answer me with your sure salvation... Do not let the floodwaters engulf me or the depths swallow me up or the pit close its mouth over me. Answer me, O Lord, out of the goodness of your love; in your great mercy turn to me. Do not hide your face from your servant; answer me quickly for I am in trouble. — Judaism[143]

He is the Compassionate, the All-Bountiful! O God, my God! Thou seest me, Thou knowest me; Thou art my Haven and my Refuge. None have I sought nor any will I seek save Thee; no path have I trodden nor any will I tread but the path of Thy love. In the darksome night of despair, my eye turneth expectant and full of hope to the morn of Thy boundless favor and at the hour of dawn my drooping soul is refreshed and strengthened in remembrance of Thy beauty and perfection. He whom the grace of Thy mercy aideth, though he be but a drop, shall become the boundless ocean, and the merest atom which the outpouring of Thy loving-kindness assisteth, shall shine even as the radiant star.

Shelter under Thy protection, O Thou Spirit of purity, Thou Whom art the All-Bountiful Provider, this enthralled, enkindled servant of Thine. Aid him in this world of being to remain steadfast and firm in Thy love and grant that this broken-winged bird attain a refuge and shelter in Thy divine nest that abideth upon the celestial tree.

— Bahá'í Faith[144]

God Fills Us with Spirit

This is my comfort in my affliction, that Thy word hath quickened me. — Judaism[145]

And the Lord God formed man of the dust of the ground, and breathed into his nostrils the breath of life; and man became a living soul. — Judaism[146]

O SON OF THE WONDROUS VISION! I have breathed within thee a breath of My own Spirit, that thou mayest be My lover. — Bahá'í Faith[147]

Do you not know that you are God's temple and that God's Spirit dwells in you? For God's temple is holy, and that temple you are. — Christianity[148]

Truly do I exist in all beings, but I am most manifest in man. The human heart is My favorite dwelling place. — Hinduism[149]

Thou hast asked Me concerning the nature of the soul. Know, verily, that the soul is a sign of God, a heavenly gem whose reality the most learned of men hath failed to grasp, and whose mystery no mind, however acute, can ever hope to unravel. It is the first among all created things to declare the excellence of its Creator, the first to recognize His glory, to cleave to His truth, and to bow down in adoration before Him. If it be faithful to God, it will reflect His light, and will, eventually, return unto Him....

— Bahá'í Faith[150]

...a spirit that is not harmed by physical ills

Know thou that the soul of man is exalted above, and is independent of all infirmities of body or mind. That a sick person showeth signs of weakness is due to the hindrances that interpose themselves between his soul and his body, for the soul itself remaineth unaffected by any bodily ailments. — Bahá'í Faith[151]

It is quite apparent to the seeing mind that a man's spirit is something very different from his physical body. The spirit is changeless, indestructible. The progress and development of the soul, the joy and sorrow of the soul, are independent of the physical body…. But if the body undergoes a change, the spirit need not be touched. When you break a glass on which the sun shines, the glass is broken, but the sun still shines! If a cage containing a bird is destroyed, the bird is unharmed! If a lamp is broken, the flame can still burn bright!

The same thing applies to the spirit of man. Though death destroy his body, it has no power over his spirit—this is eternal, everlasting, both birthless and deathless. As to the soul of man after death, it remains in the degree of purity to which it has evolved during life in the physical body, and after it is freed from the body it remains plunged in the ocean of God's Mercy.

— Bahá'í Faith[152]

God Calls Us Home

...the dust returns to the ground it came from, and the spirit returns to God who gave it.

— Judaism[153]

Let not your heart be troubled: ye believe in God, believe also in me. In my Father's house are many mansions: if it were not so, I would have told you. I go to prepare a place for you. And if I go and prepare a place for you, I will come again, and receive you unto myself; that where I am, there ye may be also. — Christianity[154]

This is what was promised for you, for everyone who turned (to God) in sincere repentance, who kept (his law), Who feared (God) Most Gracious unseen, and brought a heart turned in devotion (to Him): "Enter ye therein in Peace and Security; this is a Day of Eternal Life!" There will be for them therein all that they wish, and more besides in Our Presence. — Islam[155]

The reward for a good deed performed in this world will be enjoyed in the next world; when one waters the roots of trees fruits form at their branches. — Hinduism[156]

Whoso doeth that which is right, whether male or female, if a believer, him will we surely quicken to a happy life, and recompense them with a reward meet for their best deeds.
— Islam[157]

Those who remember me at the time of death will come to Me. Do not doubt this. Whatever occupies the mind at the time of death determines the destiny of the dying; always they will tend toward that state of being. Therefore, remember Me at all times. — Hinduism[158]

In a harbor, two ships sailed: one setting forth on a voyage, the other coming home to port. Everyone cheered the ship going out, but the ship sailing in was scarcely noticed. To this, a wise man said: "Do not rejoice over a ship setting out to sea, for you cannot know what terrible storms it may encounter and what fearful dangers it may have to endure. Rejoice rather over the ship that has safely reached port and brings its passengers home in peace."

And this is the way of the world: When a child is born, all rejoice; when someone dies, all weep. We should do the opposite. For no one can tell what trials and travails await a newborn child; but when a mortal dies in peace, we should rejoice, for he has completed a long journey, and there is no greater boon than to leave this world with the imperishable crown of a good name.

— Judaism[159]

Birth is not a beginning; death is not an end. There is existence without limitation; there is continuity without a starting point. Existence without limitation is space. Continuity without a starting point is time. There is birth, there is death, there is issuing forth, there is entering in. That through which one passes in and out without seeing its form, that is the Portal of God. — Taoism[160]

...welcoming our immortal souls

Life cannot slay. Life is not slain! Never the spirit was born; the spirit shall cease to be never; never was time it was not; End and Beginning are dreams! Birthless and deathless and changeless remaineth the spirit forever; death hath not touched it at all, dead though the house of it seems! Who knoweth it exhaustless, self-sustained, immortal, indestructible,—shall such Say,

"I have killed a man, or caused to kill?"

Nay, but as when one layeth His worn-out robes away, and, taking new ones, sayeth, "These will I wear to-day!" So putteth by the spirit lightly its garb of flesh, and passeth to inherit a residence afresh.

I say to thee weapons reach not the Life; flame burns it not, waters cannot o'erwhelm, nor dry winds wither it. Impenetrable, unentered, unassailed, unharmed, untouched, immortal, all-arriving, stable, sure, invisible, ineffable, by word And thought uncompassed, ever all itself, Thus is the Soul declared! How wilt thou, then, knowing it so, grieve when thou shouldst not grieve? How, if thou hearest that the man new-dead is, like the man new-born, still living man—One same, existent Spirit—wilt thou weep?　　— Hinduism[161]

O SON OF MAN! Thou art My dominion and My dominion perisheth not; wherefore fearest thou thy perishing? Thou art My light and My light shall never be extinguished; why dost thou dread extinction? Thou art My glory and My glory fadeth not; thou art My robe and My robe shall never be outworn. Abide then in thy love for Me, that thou mayest find Me in the realm of glory.

— Bahá'í Faith[162]

...to an eternal home

And this is the promise that he hath promised us, even eternal life. — Christianity[163]

But those who, when the law has been well preached to them, follow the law, will pass over the dominion of death, however difficult to cross. — Buddhism[164]

For our light affliction, which is but for a moment, worketh for us a far more exceeding and eternal weight of glory; While we look not at the things which are seen, but at the things which are not seen: for the things which are seen are temporal; but the things which are not seen are eternal. For we know that if our earthly house of this tabernacle were dissolved, we have a building of God, a house not made with hands, eternal in the heavens. — Christianity[165]

Never fear that old age will invade that city; never fear that this inner treasure of all reality will wither and decay. This knows no age when the body ages; this knows no dying when the body dies. This is the real city of the Creator; this is the Self, free from old age, from death and grief, hunger and thirst. In the Self all desires are fulfilled. — Hinduism[166]

Thou art now like a sear leaf, the messengers of death have come near to thee; thou standest at the door of thy departure, and thou hast no provision for thy journey.

Make thyself an island, work hard, be wise! When thy impurities art blown away, and thou art free from guilt, thou wilt enter into the heavenly world of the elect.   — Buddhism[167]

...that is gloriously different from this world

You prefer this life, although the life to come is better and more enduring.   — Islam[168]

Not like this world is the World to Come. In the World to Come there is neither eating nor drinking; no procreation of children or business transactions; no envy or hatred or rivalry; but the righteous sit enthroned, their crowns on their heads, and enjoy the luster of the Divine Splendor.   — Judaism[169]

The world beyond is as different from this world as this world is different from that of the child while still in the womb of its mother. When the soul attains the Presence of God, it will assume the form that best befits its immortality and is worthy of its celestial habitation.   — Bahá'í Faith[170]

If the dead are not raised (to another life), "Let us eat and drink, for tomorrow we die..." But someone may ask, "How are the dead raised? With what kind of body will they come?"...There are also heavenly bodies and there are earthly bodies; but the splendor of the heavenly bodies is one kind, and the splendor of the earthly bodies is another. The sun has one kind of splendor, the moon another and the stars another; and star differs from star in splendor.

So will it be with the resurrection of the dead. The body that is sown is perishable, it is raised imperishable; it is sown in dishonor, it is raised in glory; it is sown in weakness, it is raised in power; it is sown a natural body, it is raised a spiritual body. If there is a natural body, there is also a spiritual body...And just as we have borne the likeness of the earthly man, so shall we bear the likeness of the man from heaven. I declare to you, brothers, that flesh and blood cannot inherit the kingdom of God, nor does the perishable inherit the imperishable.   — Christianity[171]

No soul knoweth what joy of the eye is reserved for the good in recompense of their works.
                                        — Islam[172]

In paradise there is [no such thing as] fear;
Thou art not there, nor shrinks one from old age.
Hunger and thirst, these two transcending, Sorrow, surpassing, a man makes merry in paradise.

— Hindusim[173]

They who for my sake render him obedience,
shall all attain unto Welfare and Immortality by
the actions of the Good Spirit

— Zoroastrianism[174]

...and is more real than this world

When a man considers this world as a bubble
of froth, and as the illusion of an appearance, then
the king of death has no power over him.

— Buddhism[175]

Grieve thou not over the troubles and hardships of this nether world, nor be thou glad in
times of ease and comfort, for both shall pass away.
This present life is even as a swelling wave, or a
mirage, or drifting shadows.

...Know thou that the Kingdom is the real
world, and this nether place is only its shadow
stretching out. A shadow hath no life of its own;
its existence is only a fantasy, and nothing more;
it is but images reflected in water, and seeming as
pictures to the eye.   — Bahá'í Faith[176]

Prayers for the Departed

In all religions the belief exists that the soul survives the death of the body. Intercessions are sent up for the beloved dead, prayers are said for their progress and for the forgiveness of their sins. If the soul perished with the body all this would have no meaning. Further, if it were not possible for the soul to advance towards perfection after it had been released from the body, of what avail are all these loving prayers, of devotion?

…The very fact that our spiritual instinct, surely never given in vain, prompts us to pray for the welfare of those, our loved ones, who have passed out of the material world: does it not bear witness to the continuance of their existence? — Bahá'í Faith[177]

O God, who brought us to birth, and in whose arms we die, in our grief and shock contain and comfort us; embrace us with your love, give us hope in our confusion and grace to let go into new life.... — Christianity[178]

God full of mercy who dwells on high, grant perfect rest on the wings of Your Divine Presence in the lofty heights of the holy and pure who shine as the brightness of the heavens to the soul of [*Name of the deceased*] who has gone to his eternal rest as all his family and friends pray for the elevation of his soul. His resting place shall be in the Garden of Eden. Therefore, the Master of mercy will care for him under the protection of His wings for all time and bind his soul in the bond of everlasting life. God is his inheritance and he will rest in peace and let us say Amen.

—Judaism[179]

O my God! O Thou forgiver of sins, bestower of gifts, dispeller of afflictions!

Verily, I beseech Thee to forgive the sins of such as have abandoned the physical garment and have ascended to the spiritual world.

O my Lord! Purify them from trespasses, dispel their sorrows, and change their darkness into light. Cause them to enter the garden of happiness, cleanse them with the most pure water, and grant them to behold Thy splendors on the loftiest mount.

— Bahá'í Faith[180]

O God! Pardon our living and our dead, the present and the absent, the young and the old, the males and the females. O God! The deceased, to whom Thou accorded life, cause her to live in the observation of Islam [i.e., submission to God], and she to whom Thou gave death, cause her to die in the state of Islam. O God! Make her our forerunner, and make her, for us, a reward and a treasure, and make her, for us, a pleader, and accept her pleading.

— Islam[181]

The Lord is my shepherd; I shall not want. He maketh me to lie down in green pastures: he leadeth me beside the still waters. He restoreth my soul: he leadeth me in the paths of righteousness for his name's sake. Yea, though I walk through the valley of the shadow of death, I will fear no evil: for thou art with me; thy rod and thy staff they comfort me. Thou preparest a table before me in the presence of mine enemies: thou anointest my head with oil; my cup runneth over. Surely goodness and mercy shall follow me all the days of my life: and I will dwell in the house of the Lord for ever.

— Judaism[182]

I testify, O my Lord, that Thou hast enjoined upon men to honor their guest, and he that hath ascended unto Thee hath verily reached Thee and attained Thy Presence. Deal with him then according to Thy grace and bounty! By Thy glory, I know of a certainly that Thou wilt not withhold Thyself from that which Thou hast commanded Thy servants, nor wilt Thou deprive him that hath clung to the cord of Thy bounty and hath ascended to the Dayspring of Thy wealth.

There is none other God but Thee, the One, the Single, the Powerful, the Omniscient, the Bountiful.

— Bahá'í Faith[183]

Almighty God, you love everything you have made and judge us with infinite mercy and justice. We rejoice in your promises of pardon, joy and peace to all those who love you. In your mercy turn the darkness of death into the dawn of new life, and the sorrow of parting into the joy of heaven....

—Christian[184]

Grant, O my Lord, that they who have ascended unto Thee may repair unto Him Who is the most exalted Companion, and abide beneath the shadow of the Tabernacle of Thy majesty and the Sanctuary of Thy glory. Sprinkle, O my Lord, upon them from the ocean of Thy forgiveness what will make them worthy to abide, so long as Thine own sovereignty endureth, within Thy most exalted kingdom and Thine all-highest dominion. Potent art Thou to do what pleaseth Thee.

— Bahá'í Faith[185]

In prayer there is a mingling of station, a mingling of condition. Pray for them as they pray for you!

— Bahá'í Faith[186]

God Comforts Us

I will turn their mourning into joy, and will comfort them, and make them rejoice from their sorrow. — Judaism[187]

If you tell your sorrows to another, then he, in return, will tell you of his greater sorrows. So tell your sorrows to the Lord, your Lord and Master, who shall instantly dispel your pain.
— Sikhism[188]

Four sorts of mortals know me: he who weeps, ... and the man who yearns to know; and he who toils to help; and he who sits certain of me, enlightened. — Hinduism[189]

Those who believe and whose hearts are comforted by the mention of God—aye! By the mention of God shall their hearts be comforted, who believe and do what is right. Good cheer for them and an excellent resort. — Islam[190]

Be joyful in hope, patient in affliction, faithful in prayer. Share with God's people who are in need. Practice hospitality. Bless those who persecute you; bless and do not curse. Rejoice with those who rejoice; mourn with those who mourn. Live in harmony with one another.

— Christianity[191]

Let one live in love; let one be adept in one's duties; then joyfully one will see the end of sorrow. As the jasmine sheds its withered flowers, people should shed desire and hate....

— Buddhism[192]

O My servants! Sorrow not if, in these days and on this earthly plane, things contrary to your wishes have been ordained and manifested by God, for days of blissful joy, of heavenly delight, are assuredly in store for you. Worlds, holy and spiritually glorious, will be unveiled to your eyes. You are destined by Him, in this world and hereafter, to partake of their benefits, to share in their joys, and to obtain a portion of their sustaining grace. To each and every one of them you will, no doubt, attain.

— Bahá'í Faith[193]

Blessed are those who mourn. They will be comforted.

— Christianity [194]

The sorrows of duty,
Like the heat of the sun,
Have scorched your heart.
But let stillness fall on you,
With its sweet and cooling showers,
And you will find happiness.

— Hinduism[195]

He heals the brokenhearted, and binds up their wounds.

— Judaism[196]

If we are sick and in distress let us implore God's healing, and He will answer our prayer. When our thoughts are filled with the bitterness of this world, let us turn our eyes to the sweetness of God's compassion and He will send us heavenly calm! If we are imprisoned in the material world, our spirit can soar into the Heavens and we shall be free indeed! When our days are drawing to a close let us think of the eternal worlds, and we shall be full of joy!

— Bahá'í Faith[197]

Prayers for Serenity

God grant me the serenity to accept the things I cannot change; the courage to change the things I can; and the wisdom to know the difference.
— Christian/Interfaith[198]

Create in me a pure heart, O God; and renew a right spirit within me. Cast me not away from thy presence; and take not thy holy spirit from me. Restore unto me the joy of thy salvation; and uphold me with thy free spirit.
— Judaism[199]

I pray thee, Lord, let my way be resolute and my purpose firm in thy good counsel. Grant me, O Lord, the boon of gratefulness for thy grace, the beauty that belongs with thy worship. Give me a pure and reverent heart, uprightness of character, a tongue that speaks right and deeds that are worthy, O Lord God.
— Islam[200]

In suffering and in comfort, I meditate on You,
O Beloved.   — Sikhism[201]

Praise be to Thee, Most Supreme God, Omnipotent, Omnipresent, All-pervading, the Only
Being. Take us in Thy parental arms, raise us from
the denseness of the earth, Thy Beauty do we worship, to Thee do we give willing surrender.

Most Merciful and Compassionate God, the Idealized Lord of the whole humanity, Thee only do
we worship, and towards Thee Alone we aspire.
Open our hearts towards Thy Beauty, illuminate
our souls with Divine Light, O Thou, the Perfection of Love, Harmony and Beauty, All-powerful
Creator, Sustainer, Judge and Forgiver of our shortcomings, Lord God of the East and of the West, of
the worlds above and below, and of the seen and
unseen beings:

Pour upon us Thy Love and thy Light, give sustenance to our bodies, hearts and souls, use us
for the purpose that Thy Wisdom chooseth, and
guide us on the path of Thine Own Goodness.
Draw us closer to Thee every moment of our life,
until in us be reflected Thy Grace, Thy Glory, Thy
Wisdom, Thy Joy and Thy Peace.

                                              — Sufism[202]

Watch, dear Lord, with those who wake, or watch, or weep tonight, and give your angels charge over those who sleep. Tend your sick ones…rest your weary ones, bless your dying ones, soothe your suffering ones, pity your afflicted ones, shield your joyous ones—all for your love's sake.   — Christianity[203]

Create in me a pure heart, O my God, and renew a tranquil conscience in me, O my Hope! Through the spirit of power confirm Thou me in Thy Cause, O my Best-Beloved, and by the light of Thy glory reveal unto me Thy path, O Thou the Goal of my desire! Through the power of Thy transcendent might lift me unto the heaven of Thy holiness, O Source of my being, and by the breezes of Thine eternity gladden me, O Thou Who art my God! Let Thine everlasting melodies breathe tranquility on me, O my Companion, and let the riches of Thine ancient countenance deliver me from all except Thee, O my Master, and let the tidings of the revelation of Thine incorruptible Essence bring me joy, O Thou Who art the most manifest of the manifest and the most hidden of the hidden.

— Bahá'í Faith[204]

Gracious God, please comfort the sorrowful. When a loved one dies, it changes our lives so quickly. Help those who are living in grief to know Your loving embrace. Teach them that the dear ones they miss are truly living in the joy and peace of your heavenly kingdom. And as the pain eases and the healing begins, give them the strength to reach out to help those who follow them.

— Interfaith[205]

Remove not, O Lord, the festal board that hath been spread in Thy Name, and extinguish not the burning flame that hath been kindled by Thine unquenchable fire. Withhold not from flowing that living water of Thine that murmureth with the melody of Thy glory and Thy remembrance, and deprive not Thy servants from the fragrance of Thy sweet savors breathing forth the perfume of Thy love.

Lord! Turn the distressing cares of Thy holy ones into ease, their hardship into comfort, their abasement into glory, their sorrow into blissful joy, O Thou that holdest in Thy grasp the reins of all mankind!

Thou art, verily, the One, the Single, the Mighty, the All-Knowing, the All-Wise.

— Bahá'í Faith[206]

Every thought of my mind, every emotion of my heart, every movement of my being, every feeling and every sensation, each cell of my body, each drop of my blood—all, all is yours, yours absolutely, yours without reserve, you can decide my life or my death, my happiness or my sorrow, my pleasure or my pain. Whatever you do with me, whatever comes to me from you, will lead me to the Divine Rapture. — Hinduism[207]

Lord, there are many such, dwelling in narrow resentments, embittered by wrongs others have inflicted, confined to harsh enmities, imprisoned in spirit by despair at evil deeds, drained of hope and bereft of peace, left to great hatred in this world. Have mercy, good Lord, upon all these whose world, through human malice, despairs of human kindness. Judge and turn their oppressors. Release again, for the fearful, the springs of trust and goodness. Give them liberty of heart—the liberty of those who leave room for the judgment of God.

Enlarge our hearts, O God, that we may do battle against evil and bear the sorrows of the weary, and seek and serve thy will. Great art thou, O Lord. There is naught that is a match for thee. O my Lord, enlarge my heart. — Islam[208]

Lord, may all be happy. O Lord grant happiness to all of us. May no one be unhappy. May all be healthy and possess all the good things of life. May all of us see goodness everywhere and all follow the path of virtue and righteousness. May all your creation be happy and no one be miserable.
— Hinduism[209]

REFERENCES

We have tried to trace and acknowledge ownership of copyright. We apologize if we inadvertently overlooked any rights or omitted any required credits. We will be happy to make appropriate arrangements with any copyright holder we have been unable to contact. The Bahá'í Writings, whose translations are still under copyright, were used with permission of the National Spiritual Assembly of the Bahá'ís of the United States.

1 Tanakh, Psalms 121
2 Qur'án 2:186
3 Bible, Matthew 11:28–30
4 Selections from the Writings of 'Abdu'l-Bahá, p. 51
5 Shri Guru Granth Sahib, Section 7 — Raag Gauree
6 The Hindu Prayer Book
7 Shri Guru Granth Sahib, Section 40 — Shaloks Of
   Devotee Kabeer Jee
8 Bible, Matthew 7:7–8
9 Shri Guru Granth Sahib, Section 7 — Raag Gauree
10 Qur'án 8: 9
11 The Báb, Bahá'í Prayers, U.S. 2002 ed., p. 227
12 Methodist Book of Offices (Words to Comfort, Words
   to Heal, p. 119)
13 Shri Guru Granth Sahib, Section 14 — Raag
   Dhanaasaree
14 The Hindu Prayer Book
15 The Báb, Bahá'í Prayers, U.S. 2002 ed., pg. 226
16 Rig-Veda, *The Vedic Experience*, edited and translated by
   Raimundo Panikkar (Los Angeles: University of
   California Press, 1977), p. 72.
17 http://www.viha.ca/spiritual_care/prayers.htm
18 Bible, 1 John 4:8
19 Tanakh, Genesis 1:31
20 Bahá'u'lláh, Arabic Hidden Words #3, #4
21 Shri Guru Granth Sahib, Section 5 — Siree Raag
22 Bhagavad Gita, 9 (Edwin Arnold tr.)
23 Bhagavad Gita, 18 (Edwin Arnold tr.)
24 Qur'án 26:77–82

25 Tanakh, Psalms 145:8–9

26 Bible, Luke 12:27–31

27 Bhagavad Gita, 10 (Edwin Arnold tr.)

28 'Abdu'l-Bahá, The Promulgation of Universal Peace, p. 214

29 Tanakh, Psalms 100:1–101:1

30 Qur'án 13:23

31 Dhammapada—Sayings of the Buddha 2 (J. Richards tr.)

32 Bhagavad Gita, 9 (Edwin Arnold tr.)

33 http://www.prayerinamerica.org/prayer-directory/prayer-and-social-justice/

34 Islam: Common Prayer, p. 41

35 'Abdu'l-Bahá, Bahá'í Prayers, p. 33

36 www.prayers-for-special-help.com/Prayers-for-Children.html

37 'Abdu'l-Bahá, Bahá'í Prayers, p. 28

38 Common Prayer, p. 102

39 Bahá'u'lláh: Gleanings from the Writings of Bahá'u'lláh, p. 301

40 Selections from the Writings of the Báb, p. 94

41 'Abdu'l-Bahá, Bahá'í Prayers, p. 64

42 Qur'án, 64:11

43 Tanakh, Exodus 15:26

44 The Teaching of the Buddha, p. 78

46 Shri Guru Granth Sahib, Section 25 — Raag Maaroo

46 Bahá'u'lláh: Gleanings from the Writings of Bahá'u'lláh, p. 155

47 Book of Prayer, p. 103

48 Qur'án 1:1–7

49 Lotus Prayer Book, p. 153

50 The Báb, Bahá'í Prayers, p.227

51 The Hindu Prayer Book

52 http://www.prayerinamerica.org/prayer-directory/prayer-and-social-justice/

53 'Abdu'l-Bahá, The Promulgation of Universal Peace, p. 301

54 Qur'án 3:31

55 Bible, Mark 3:28

56 Tanakh, Isaiah 55:6–7

57 Bhagavad Gita (Edwin Arnold tr.)

58 Selections from the Writings of 'Abdu'l-Bahá, p. 232

59 Bible, Matthew 6:9–13

60 Tanakh, Psalms 25:15–21

61 Qur'an 2:286

62 The Wisdom of Judaism, p. 231

63 'The Báb, Bahá'í Prayers, p. 227

64 Abdu'l-Bahá, Bahá'í Prayers, p. 82

65 Tanakh, Psalms 27:1

66 Qur'án 4:171

67 Bahá'u'lláh, Gems of Divine Mysteries, p. 60

68 Tanakh, Proverbs 1:33

69 Qur'án 59:22–23

70 Bahá'u'lláh, Arabic Hidden Words #9

71 Ashtavakra Gita 11:5

72 Tanakh, Psalms 71:2–6

73 Shri Guru Granth Sahib, Section 11 — Raag Bihaagra

74 Vedas, Rig Veda — Book 1

75 'Abdu'l-Bahá, Bahá'í Prayers, p. 135

76 Book of Prayer, p. 108

77 The Báb, Bahá'í Prayers, p. 132

78 The Hindu Prayer Book

79 Qur'án 26:80

80 Tanakh, Jeremiah 30:17

81 Shri Guru Granth Sahib, Section 27 — Raag Kaydaaraa

82 Bahá'u'lláh, Bahá'í Prayers, p. 87

83 Zend-Avesta, Khorda Avesta — Book of Common Prayer, pt. 1

84 Tanakh, Psalms 30:2

85 Shri Guru Granth Sahib, Section 7 — Raag Gauree

86 Bible, James 5:13–16

87 Shri Guru Granth Sahib, Section 30 — Raag Saarang

88 Tanakh, Psalms 107:19–21

89 'Abdu'l-Bahá, Selections from the Writings of 'Abdu'l-Bahá, p. 151

90 Zend-Avesta, Khorda Avesta — Book of Common Prayer, pt. 1

91 http://www.angelfire.com/md/elanmichaels/
physician.html

92 Vinaya, Mahavagga 8:26.3

93 Tanakh, Proverbs 16:24

94 'Abdu'l-Bahá, Selections from the Writings of 'Abdu'l-
Bahá, pp. 150–151

95 'Abdu'l-Bahá, Selections from the Writings of 'Abdu'l-
Bahá, #139

96 Book of Prayer, p. 128

97 http://theonlinemuslim.blogspot.com/2008/01/
prayers-and-healing.html

98 Bahá'u'lláh, Bahá'í Prayers, p. 87

99 Shri Guru Granth Sahib, Section 13 — Raag Sorat'h

100 http://www.allaboutprayer.org/healing-prayers.htm

101 The Hindu Prayer Book

102 http://www.angelfire.com/md/elanmichaels/
buddpeace.html

103 http://www.duas.org/general_dua.htm

104 Bahá'u'lláh, Prayers and Meditations, p. 265

105 http://www.ourcatholicfaith.org/prayer/p-
healing.html

106 Common Prayer, p. 64

107 Bahá'u'lláh, Bahá'í Prayers, p. 87

108 http://www.duas.org/general_dua.htm

109 Tanakh, Psalms 6:2

110 http://www.sufiorder.org/prayers_4.html

111 Bible, Romans 5:3–5

112 Dalai Lama

113 Qur'án 2:150–152

114 Tanakh, Isaiah 30:20–21

115 Shri Guru Granth Sahib, Section 34 — Raag
Prabhaatee

116 Shri Guru Granth Sahib, Section 8 — Raag Aasaa

117 'Abdu'l-Bahá, Star of the West, vol. 14, no. 2, p. 41

118 Qur'án, 2:153

119 Bible, James 1:2–4

120 Bahá'u'lláh, Gleanings from the Writings of
Bahá'u'lláh, p. 129

121 Dhammapada — Sayings of the Buddha 2 (J. Richards tr.)
122 Shri Guru Granth Sahib, Section 22 — Raag Raamkalee
123 'Abdu'l-Bahá, Paris Talks, p. 178
124 Bhagavad Gita 2:61–65
125 Shri Guru Granth Sahib, Section 5 — Siree Raag
126 Bahá'u'lláh, Bahá'u'lláh and the New Era, p. 108
127 Dalai Lama
128 Ashtavakra Gita 11:1
129 Tanakh, Proverbs 17:22
130 Tao Te Ching, #46
131 Qur'án 29:2–3
132 Bible, Mark 11:23–4
133 Dalai Lama
134 'Abdu'l-Bahá, Paris Talks, pp. 50–51
135 Dalai Lama
136 Bible, Matthew 25: 34–40 '
137 Abdu'l-Bahá, The Promulgation of Universal Peace, p. 204
138 Common Prayer, p. 42
139 Bahá'u'lláh, Prayers and Meditations, p. 78–79
140 Common Prayer, p. 30
141 Rig Veda — Book 6
142 Common Prayer, p. 58
143 Tanakh, Psalms 69
144 'Abdu'l-Bahá, Bahá'í Prayers, p. 29
145 Tanakh, Psalms 119:50
146 Tanakh, Genesis 2:7
147 Bahá'u'lláh, Arabic Hidden Words #19
148 Bible, 1 Corinthians 3:16–17
149 Srimad Bhagavatam, 11.2
150 Bahá'u'lláh, Gleanings from the Writings of Bahá'u'lláh, p. 158
151 Bahá'u'lláh, Gleanings from the Writings of Bahá'u'lláh, LXXX
152 'Abdu'l-Bahá, Paris Talks, pp. 65–66
153 Tanakh, Ecclesiastes 12:7

154 Bible, John 14:1
155 Qur'án 50:32–35
156 The Wisdom of Hinduism, p. 44
157 Qur'án 16:97
158 Bhagavad Gita 8.5–7
159 Talmud (Words to Comfort, Words to Heal, p. 60)
160 Chang Tzu, 23
161 Bhagavad Gita, Chapter 2
162 Bahá'u'lláh, Arabic Hidden Words #14
163 Bible, 1 John 2:25
164 Dhammapada 6:86
165 Bible, 1 John 2:25
166 Chandogya Upanishad
167 Dhammapada 18:235–6
168 Qur'án 87:16–17
169 Talmud
170 Bahá'u'lláh, Gleanings from the Writings of
    Bahá'u'lláh, p. 81
171 Bible, 1 Corinthians 15:32–50
172 Qur'án 32:17
173 Katha Upanishad
174 Zend-Avesta, Avesta — Yasna
175 Dhammapada 170–71 (The Wisdom of Buddhism, p.
    110)
176 'Abdu'l-Bahá, Selections from the Writings of
    'Abdu'l-Bahá, p. 177–8
177 'Abdu'l-Bahá, Paris Talks, p. 89
178http://www.cofe.anglican.org/worship/liturgy/
    commonworship/texts/funeral/
    prayers.html#thanksgiving
179http://www.prayer-and-prayers.info/funeral-prayers/
    jewish-funeral-prayer.htm
180 'Abdu'l-Bahá, Bahá'í Prayers, p. 44
181 http://www.explorefaith.org/prayer/essays/
    worldPrayer2.html]
182 Tanakh, Psalms 23:1–6
183 Bahá'u'lláh, Bahá'í Prayers, p. 43

184 http://www.cofe.anglican.org/worship/liturgy/
      commonworship/texts/funeral/
      prayers.html#thanksgiving]
185 Bahá'u'lláh, Prayers and Meditations, p. 279
186 'Abdu'l-Bahá, 'Abdu'l-Bahá in London, p. 95
187 Tanakh, Jeremiah 31:12
188 Shri Guru Granth Sahib, Section 21 — Raag Gond
189 Bhagavad Gita (Edwin Arnold tr.)
190 Qur'án 13:28
191 Bible, Romans 12:12–16
192 Dhammapada — Sayings of the Buddha 2 (J.
      Richards tr.)
193 Bahá'u'lláh, Gleanings from the Writings of
      Bahá'u'lláh, p. 329
194 Bible, Matthew 5:4
195 Ashtavakra Gita 18:3
196 Tanakh, Psalms 147:3
197 'Abdu'l-Bahá, Paris Talks, p. 111
198 Attributed to Reinhold Niebuhr, a Protestant Theo-
      logian, but adapted and adopted by Alcoholics
      Anonymous and used by people of all faiths.
199 Tanakh, Psalms 51:10–12
200 Book of Prayer, p. 43
201 Shri Guru Granth Sahib, Section 6 — Raag Maajh
202 http://www.sufiorder.org/prayers.html
203 Book of Prayer, p. 178
204 Bahá'u'lláh, Bahá'í Prayers, p. 142
205 http://www.stmarcelline.com/
      PrayersforBlessing.htm#Grieving
206 'Abdu'l-Bahá, Bahá'í Prayers, p. 22
207 Bhagavata Purana, Book of Prayer, p. 68
208 Common Prayer, p. 73
209 The Hindu Prayer Book

Please add your own favorite prayers and meditations on these pages, and may God bless you.

Made in United States
Troutdale, OR
08/16/2023

12126479R00056